STICK IN THE SIX

A Winding Journey Through The Soul Of A Cancer Survivor

Jorge Sousa

Tellwell Talent

www.tellwell.ca

ISBN

978-1-77302-566-7 (Paperback)

978-1-77302-567-4 (eBook)

DEDICATION

This book is dedicated to all the fighters, survivors, care-givers, doctors, families, friends and fallen that have been or are being affected by this disease.

"Embrace the pain and burn it as fuel for the ride."
– Kenji Miyazawa

TABLE OF CONTENTS

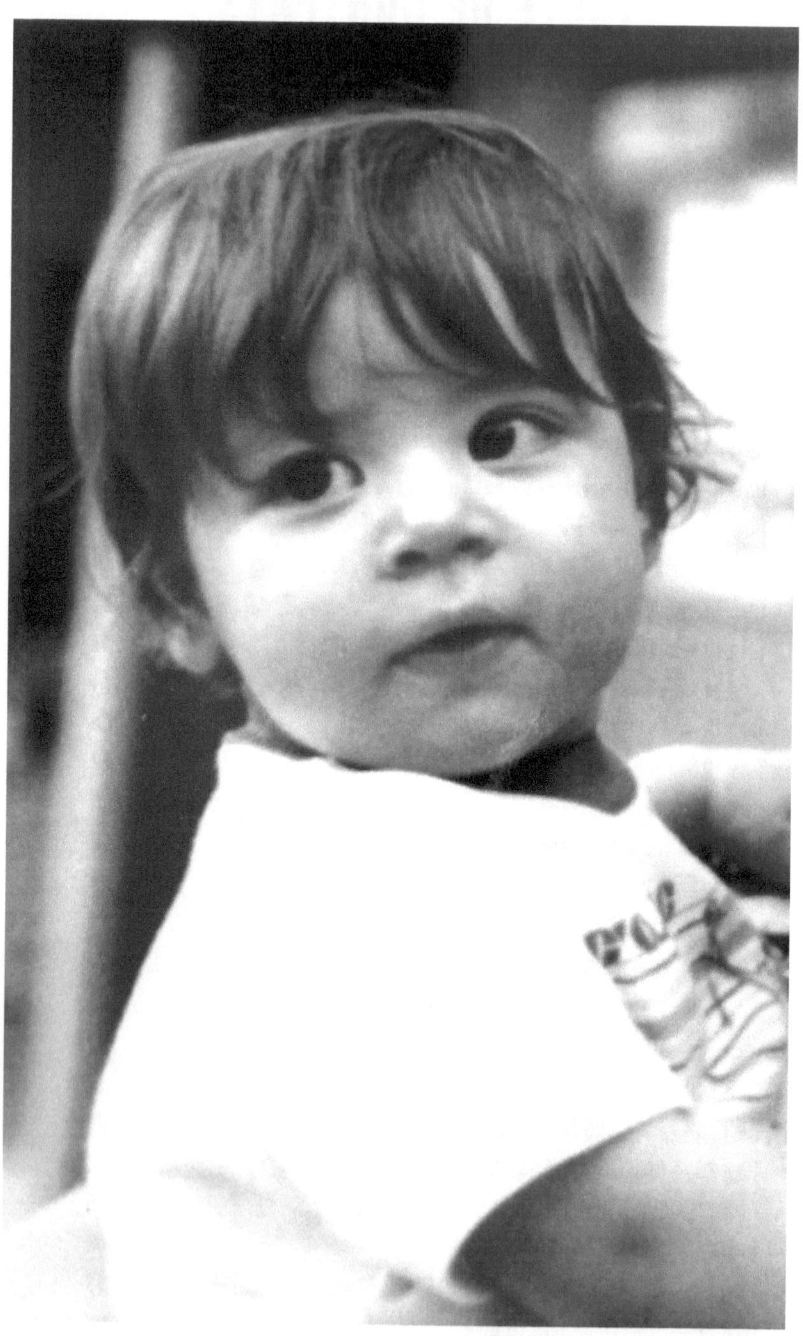

TURN 1
IT ALL STARTS SOMEWHERE

*** DISCLAIMER TO THE READER ***

The language, views and opinions expressed in this book are those of the author and do not necessarily reflect the official position of any person(s) mentioned within. Assumptions made within this story are not meant to make an "ASS" out of "YOU" and "ME," but rather to entertain and hopefully provide some life lessons.

Where does every good story start?

I'd say at the beginning but that would be a HUGE lie! It all starts with an idea, a light bulb going off in your dome, a moment of clarity, if you will. This crazy idea started somewhere in 2013 but it really goes back way further than that.

I was born and raised right here in the "6ix," the "T-Dot," "Hogtown," the "Big Smoke" or for you out-of-towners, Toronto, Ontario, Canada, in the summer of 1977. A time when the Toronto Blue Jays were in their inaugural season at Exhibition Stadium. (For the record it snowed on opening day.) It had only been ten years since the Toronto Maple Leafs won the Stanley Cup, the Toronto Raptors weren't even a twinkle in the NBA's eye, at 301 Front Street West the world's tallest free-standing structure had been erected less than a year prior and, sadly, the world lost the "King" while he was sitting on *la toilette*.

Times were different indeed and, yet, so many things still seem to be the same.

The Toronto Blue Jays (while having won back-to-back championships) are now dealing with a new president in his inaugural season at the helm (Good luck, Shapiro), the Toronto Maple Leafs have not won a Stanley Cup now in almost fifty years, the Raptors are still just a twinkle in the NBA's eye (even though we rake in a shit ton of money for them considering they are the only Canadian team) and, sadly, we lost another "King" (this one of Pop) a few years back while he was allegedly sleeping.

So what the hell does this have to do with me being sick in the 6ix? Nothing really. I was just providing you with some context and, in all honesty, they're my words and thoughts so suck it up, buttercup!

Okay, so I said my story started in 2013 but, actually, the summer of 2012 is where it all really began. It was July 18, 2012, to be more accurate. It was a Wednesday and the sun was shining as it often does. I woke from my slumber and got out of bed (I lived right downtown at the time), hopped into the shower and started my day. Not feeling a hundred per cent over the past couple of weeks, I noticed that morning that my hand was swollen and sore and thought maybe I had been bitten by a spider or had an allergic reaction to something from the night before. I got ready for work as always, fired up the motorcycle and rode off to the office. By 9:00 a.m., I was on my way to St. Joseph's hospital (yes, I rode myself to the hospital) as I knew something was up with my arm. Did I mention it was my left arm? Within twenty minutes of registering with the triage nurse, I was being pushed through emerge and given blood thinners, having an ultrasound and X-rays done on my chest and, last but not least, getting a CT scan for dessert. B-E-A-utiful!

For the record, I hate hospitals: the smells, the sights, the sounds, the death in the air, none of it is appealing to me and at this point it was around 4:00 p.m. Truth be told, I was scared shitless but at least I knew why my arm was swollen. (Way to look on the bright side, asshole.) I had a blood clot in my left arm, which explained the swelling and stiffness but didn't really explain why I hadn't been feeling a hundred per cent for the past couple of weeks.

The doctors were concerned that I may have had a PE or pulmonary embolism (for you out-of-towners who have never heard of a PE before, it is a blockage of an artery in the lungs) and they kept asking me if I had felt any chest pain, if I understood why I was there, etc. (When did this become an interview?) I was at the end of my rope and had completed all my tests and my partner at the time was now at the hospital with me. She worked nights as a critical care nurse and it was "critical" she be there when we spoke with the doctor. As we waited in the designated waiting area, I started to get this sinking feeling that there was more going on than just a plain old blood clot in my arm, and man-oh-man was I right.

TURN 2
IF IT AIN'T BROKE...

Now where were we?

Ah, yes, the designated waiting area. Okay, so while I waited in the emergency area for the doctor to see me, I had a million things running through my head and they went a little something like this:

1. *If I have to be here longer than one night, who the hell is going to take my motorcycle home?*

2. *I have band practice tomorrow…shit, I'm going to have to cancel that (www.desolaterage.com)!*

3. *What about work? We're in the middle of a project and I have meetings scheduled for tomorrow and Friday.*

4. *I have hockey on Friday night…oh well, they're
    going to have to find another goalie.*

5. *My birthday is coming up and there are celebra-
    tions to be had, dammit!*

6. *Maybe it's just an allergy and I'll get some meds
    and go home.*

7. *WHAT IS THAT SMELLL?*

At some point I heard a voice calling my name over the ramblings
in my head.

"Yeah, that's me," I responded.

"Is there a Mr. Sousa here?"

This prick just walked by me, calling my name again and didn't
hear me the first time.

"Yes! That's me," I responded yet again.

At this point he looked me up and down as if I had two heads or
was part of the Walking Dead. He seemed surprised that I was
even upright and able to speak.

"Come with me," he said while shrugging his shoulders and we
were off to the races.

We walked into this little room and the doctor closed the glass
door and curtain behind us and began with the inquisition once
more, for good measure.

"Do you know why you're here today?" he asked.

We went back and forth for a while about why I thought I was
there and he asked a whole mess of questions:

1. *Had I been tired a lot lately? No more than usual.*

2. *Had I been eating properly? Sure.*

3. *Any weight loss? Yeah, but that happens when you play sports four times a week, doesn't it?*

4. *Did I have night sweats? Not that I was aware of.*

5. *Was I short of breath? A little but only during physical activity.*

6. *Any funny lumps on my body? Nope.*

7. *Did I smoke? Not anymore. (I had quit on June 1, 2012.)*

8. *Had I been sick often? Yes, more than usual during that year.*

So after the inquisition was over and the poking and prodding was complete, the doctor proceeded to tell us that there were two possible diagnoses for what they had uncovered. It sounded to me as if he was about to ask me if I wanted to play "Let's Make a Deal" and choose Door Number One or Door Number Two. One of the possibilities was something that he had only read about in a book and about 0.5 per cent of the world's population had been diagnosed with. (Being the type of person I am, that actually sounded appealing to me for a split second!)

The other, well...

Have you ever seen the movie *50/50* with Seth Rogen and Joseph Gordon-Levitt? It's supposed to be a comedy but I think it's a great balance between drama and comedy and really hits home on various levels. There's a moment in the movie when Joseph Gordon-Levitt's character, Adam, goes to see his doctor and he is told that he has been diagnosed with the Big C. The doctor continues speaking to him but in that moment after being given his diagnosis, the world fades to grey and there's a high-pitched ringing that is heard, drowning everything out.

This is where it all begins, my friends.

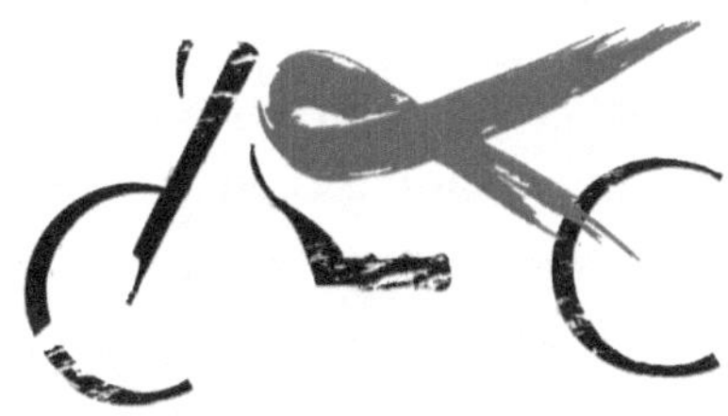

TURN 3
THIS WAS JUST A TEST

"This is a test. SICK IN THE 6IX *is conducting a test of the Emergency Broadcast System. This is only a test. If this had been an actual emergency, the attention signal you just heard would have been followed by official information, news, or instructions. We are currently experiencing technical difficulties and will resume our regularly scheduled program momentarily."*
<END TEST HERE>

And, we're back to our regularly scheduled program already in progress! So, there I was in a little fish bowl in the emergency room at St. Joe's Hospital listening to some doctor go on about lumps and bumps.

Meanwhile in my head there was an entire bargaining session going about how I could make my way out of this and just hop on the bike and ride off. I swear I heard more words than just lymphoma but with a blank stare I said, "What?"

My partner looked at me very concerned and reiterated the one thing that I dreaded to hear. Now I don't know about you but there is really only one word to describe the feeling at that specific moment. For those with virgin eyes skip over this part, okay?

FUCK!!!!!!!!!!!!!!!!!!!!!!!!!!!!!!!! (I'm sure my mother will be thrilled about this.)

There you have it, folks, thirty-four years and 350 days of being on this planet and I was standing there in complete shock with absolutely nothing to say, which to some may be unbelievable. I had what people call an out-of-body experience. At that moment, it was as if I was watching my life in 4K. I remember looking around the room and seeing the beige curtain with flowers on it that the doctor had pulled over to provide us with privacy, hearing the buzzing of the fluorescent hospital lights, taking stock of the faded yellowish paint on the wall and the noises going on outside of the room. Every second felt like an eternity and my breathing had gone from a semi-normal pace to a rushed, gasping-for-every-breath-I-could-take kind of speed.

The floor felt as if it was dropping out from below me, and nothing seemed real. I do recall the doctor asking me if I understood what he was talking about and if I wanted a moment to collect my thoughts. NO…YOU THINK?

One of the funniest moments during this whole ordeal was when the doctor asked me if I wanted a prescription for some drugs to help me relax and I shook my head "no" while my partner standing behind me was nodding "yes." Ativan is by far the best thing ever! Of course with every dark cloud there is a silver lining, and while my situation was not great, all hope was not lost and we were going to fight this come hell or high water. The doctor told us that in approximately ninety per cent of cases my type of cancer was treatable, if not curable, so the next step would be to find out how bad the situation really was.

TURN 4
NEXT STOP, SHITSVILLE!

Let's recap for a second:

It was a Wednesday in July, I felt like garbage, I rode my motor-cycle to a hospital that was much farther than the one my partner worked at, found out I had a blood clot in my left arm, completed a ton of tests, was scared out of my mind with the news I'd been given, still didn't know what was going to happen next, now had to call someone to pick up my motorcycle as I was on blood thin-ners, probably wouldn't ride for the foreseeable future (it would be almost eighteen months before I did so again), was embarking on a journey I had zero interest in starting and, to top it off, I still didn't know how bad the situation was! At least I could go home and freak out on my own turf.

Caught up? Okay, let's continue...

So at this point it was now early evening and I was going to have to contact my father in hopes that he would be able to come to the hospital and pick up my bike, as riding was now out of the question. This was going to be the start of many long journeys to and from the hospital on a more-regular-than-I'd-like basis and, if you've read this far, you already know how much I hate hospitals. Both my partner and I went outside and she called her parents/sister/work to give them the wonderful news while I contacted my father. While we waited, I thought it might be best to send work an email just to let them know I wouldn't be in for the rest of the week.

> *Sent: July 18, 2012 9:35:16 p.m.*
>
> *Hi team,*
>
> *Just wanted to further update you on what's happening. I will be going back to the hospital for the next couple of days to address the clot in my arm and will be seeing a specialist for the CT scan (hopefully tomorrow). I will keep you posted but probably won't be back for the rest of the week. Thanks again for all the support.*

Now that work had an update and was aware that I wouldn't be in for the remainder of the week and my father was on his way, I could focus on FREAKING OUT! I mean, focus on dealing with the issue(s) at hand. It was time to head to the pharmacy to get my prescription and then go home to prepare for Round Two.

I would have to go back to the hospital on a daily basis to receive blood thinners for my arm, which in my case would require getting needles. Just like I'm not a fan of hospitals, I'm also not a fan of needles and, yes, while I realize that I have tattoos, it's a different type of needle and a totally different set of circumstances, as well. Little did I know that for the next ten months I'd have to inject myself with two needles every morning, which was just bloody fantastic!

The next morning, once I finished up in emergency with the blood thinners, I decided I'd make my way up to the sixth floor to visit the oncology ward and get this bad boy rolling by setting up an appointment with the oncologist. It was time to find out what was going in this boy's body. I took the elevator upstairs, got to the reception desk and was pleasantly greeted by one of the nicest people I have ever had the pleasure of meeting.

"May I help you?" she asked

"I'm here to…" My voice failed me and I FREAKED OUT.

Tears rolled down my face and I must have turned a nice shade of ghostly gray (which is an actual colour in any Benjamin Moore swatch – KM4884). Once I mellowed out, I booked an appointment to see the oncologist for the next morning and was off to the races. What was coming my way next was way beyond what I ever thought I could handle, but somehow did.

(I should probably clarify something here: During most of this ordeal my mother was the only person who had not been notified of what had been going on and for that I'm sorry, but there was nothing that she was going to be able to do and there was no need to worry her while she was thousands of miles away in another country. I realize it was probably a really shitty thing to do but, if I had to do it over again, I wouldn't change a thing…hardly.)

TURN 5
ROUND TWO

There we were on a beautiful Friday morning making our way, once again, to the hospital's emergency unit for another dose of blood thinners and—to make my day as fantastic as possible— a quick jaunt to the sixth floor to meet with the oncologist and discuss what the plan was going forward. This routine of travelling to the emergency department and having to explain my situation over and over was getting old and I was beginning to get a little punchy. I realize now that it was for my own good.

We made our way up to the sixth floor and waited for the oncologist to see us. While I love my pops and he is usually great at diffusing situations that are stressful, it felt as if he was having the opposite effect on me this time. I was in such a frantic state that the Dalai Lama himself could have been there trying to calm me down and I probably would've snapped at him. The nurse called out my number in much the same way as the electronic message boards at the passport office that tell you what kiosk to go to, and away we went into the oncologist's office.

Before I continue, I just want to put it out there that there is a right way to speak with people dealing with a tremendous amount of stress and there is a not-so-right way. Guess which approach this oncologist took?

This lady was a complete nightmare! She was harsh, aggressive, cold, and couldn't give two shits that I was freaking out and in a constant state of hyperventilation. Thankfully, she would not be my regular oncologist. It became a back-and-forth discussion between her, my partner and my father. Ultimately, she told us that I would need to be admitted to the hospital immediately so that they could perform tests (a biopsy) to confirm what was suspected and at what stage the cancer was at. My brain instantly went back to the bargaining table and I tried to weasel my way out of being admitted to emergency. Being admitted would mean waiting because they didn't have a timeline for when I would be having the biopsy.

"It will be sometime between today and Monday," she said.

Oh, well ...then that's okay, because I really didn't have any plans for the weekend anyway.

Her recommendation was that I admit myself to emergency, but she was leaving it up to me. HA! Up to me...really? We left her office and returned to the waiting area while the oncologist got the paperwork ready for me to take to emergency. By now it was mid-morning and all I wanted to do was go home. I had no interest in re-admitting myself and battled with my partner and dad on the next steps. I recall saying to them over and over, "I just want to go home!" But, to no avail. I wasn't going to be given that option this time.

Now, I considered myself one of the fortunate souls on this planet, having never been admitted to a hospital for more than a few hours before that point in time. This was going to be a new experience for me and not one I was looking forward to facing. It would test my patience and sanity on more than one occasion over the next couple of days.

TURN 6
...AND SO WE WAIT

And…go! This was the first of many hurry-up-and-wait moments I would face over the next couple of days. We made our way to the emergency area and once again I met with the triage nurse to be re-admitted. What I don't recall being told was that I would have to wait in the emergency area all goddamn day. I'm not lying to you; it was literally the entire day.

There was a lot of time spent just being static and it was a kind of siege mentality for most of the day. Every few hours I'd see a nurse or doctor and the conversation would always be the same and it would go a little something like this:

"We're in the process of trying to find you a room," they'd say.

"Great! Do we know when I will meet with the thoracic surgeon?" I'd ask.

"No, they are still trying to find a time slot on the list for when to perform the biopsy."

This happened on numerous occasions during the day. The best part was that because they weren't sure if I was going under the knife on that day or the next, I was told that I couldn't eat or drink until they figured their shit out. FANTASTIC! (I really wasn't hungry, but a beverage would've been nice.) Once they found a vein, I was given an IV to tide me over until after the surgery. It was a complete nightmare.

Let me explain what the plan was. I would be on the wait list for a biopsy and the thoracic surgeon was going to try and find some time during the next couple of days to slice open my neck, run a tube down into my chest and then remove a few sample lymph nodes so that they could analyse them to fully understand what they were dealing with. Cue hyperventilation!

I was going to have to let work know I wouldn't be in for the next few days. I could be waiting here awhile before this massacre began or the doctors gave me a straight answer. So I sent them an email:

> *Sent: July 21, 2012 1:11:13 p.m.*
>
> *Hi everyone,*
>
> *Just wanted to give you an update as to how I'm feeling and what's going on. The CT scan apparently showed something that they are concerned about and I will require more tests on Monday and Tuesday. I will be back in the office on Wednesday and hopefully will have a few more answers then.*
>
> *As for me, I'm trying to stay positive and my arm seems to be better.*

Oh yeah, I almost forgot—my arm was much better and my sausage-sized fingers were slowly going back to normal.

TURN 7
MOTORCYCLE MADNESS

For those of you who don't know me or my family (specifically my grandfather, dad and uncle) we have the propensity to speak to random strangers, usually of the opposite sex. Since I was going to be stuck in the emergency area with nothing to do but wait for the doctors to have their Thunder Dome moment and figure out what to do with me, I thought I'd have a quick chat with anyone who would be willing to listen.

As I've mentioned before, my father has a great way of knowing how to diffuse any stressful situation with a bit of humour or distraction and, as always, he was able to do so by sparking up a conversation with the woman sitting beside me. I don't know if it was her motorcycle jacket, helmet or the fact that she also in a great amount of pain, but for a brief moment I was grateful for the distraction. There we were chatting about bikes and stuff. Turns out she had been in a motorcycle accident when she was younger and had lost part of her right leg. Now, she had been in another one and was waiting to get an X-ray to see if she had broken something on the same leg *(...and I thought my situation sucked!)*.

After a while, my partner's parents showed up from London, Ontario, to support us and keep us company. It was a revolving door of people hanging out with me trying to keep calm while I waited to see a doctor or nurse.

My IV bag was running on empty and so was my patience for all of this shit! I must have been a miserable prick to be around those first couple of days. While I really don't remember what my attitude was like I probably owe a ton of people an apology for acting the way I did. This wasn't your usual routine checkup or "we'll have you on your way" type of situation.

I had been poked and prodded (and not in the good way) by nurses and doctors for the last three days and was now in limbo waiting for this magical biopsy. Speaking of poking...have you ever had a nurse miss your vein and then go to flush it? Not fun, but in hindsight it was pretty amusing to see the nurse freak out as the spot on my hand blew up when she tried to flush the vein that she had missed.

It was now dinner time and I was getting HANGRY! This was a bad Mac Combo but there was light at the end of this tunnel...maybe...

TURN 8
TWO HUNDRED-PLUS BEATS PER MINUTE

According to the National Institute of Health, the average resting heart rate in adults is sixty to one hundred beats per minute. Keep that statistic in mind.

I spent the entire day watching people come and go, met with a few doctors, but we still didn't have a time table for my biopsy and because everything was up in the air they just sort of had me on ice until they figured out what the plan was. At around 9:00 p.m., with no food, an IV attached to my hand and no idea when I was going to get moved from the emergency area, I realized that I had spent the day trying to learn how to become a Zen Master. (I don't think I did a very good job.)

At some point a few doctors finally greeted me and told me that they had a bed for little ole me and that I would probably be having the procedure done during the night or early morning. The thoracic surgeon would be in to see me and discuss the procedure in greater detail.

Ladies and gentlemen, we have lift-off—or at least the go-no-go from mission control to get this mother started but, alas, these false starts would be the norm over the next few hours.

The orderly escorted me to the area where I would be laying my head down for the night. The nurse came by, changed the IV bag and decided that now would be a good time to take some blood.

As I've mentioned before, I don't do well with needles and, to top it off, I had this weird thing about them trying to remove blood from my left arm, blood clot and all. They had had difficulty finding useful veins (they hide when they know they're going to be poked) and the ones in my hands were currently being occupied, or had been, and I was feeling a little bit like a pincushion. The nurse unsuccessfully tried a few times to remove my precious blood and then decided that while we waited for a technician, it would make sense to check my vitals.

It must have scared the shit out of this lady once she put the heart rate monitor on me...ready? Two hundred and twenty-one beats per minute while resting! Clearly I was coming apart at the seams and it didn't look as if I was going to calm down anytime soon. The technician came in and within a few seconds found a vein, removed whatever blood she needed and left. That was easy.

Around 11:00 p.m. one of the resident doctors came in to see me to let me know that the biopsy would not happen that evening and that the thoracic surgeon would be in to discuss my situation later on in the night or early morning as they were still debating on how to handle my biopsy. (Way to make someone feel good about this whole thing, folks). After a quick verbal chess game about the IV staying in, I asked if I could eat something as the procedure was not going to happen anytime soon, and with a smile the doctor agreed to my "demands."

In my head there was only one response…

"Thank you, thank you, thank you! Now get this shit out of my hand and let's get some food up in this joint!"

I thanked the doctor and asked anyone and everyone that would listen if there was any food left over from dinner time. The nice nurse said she would go and check. She returned with what I can only describe as the BEST tuna fish and egg salads sandwiches I have ever eaten in my life!

Seriously…they were delicious!

TURN 9
A WIN FOR THE GOOD GUYS

Have you ever seen a yo-yo work?

This, folks, would be what most of my night would be like after those delicious sandwiches and juice. Every hour a nurse would check in on me and want to take blood, a resident doctor would come by and let me know that they were still debating with one another about how to handle my situation and then I'd hyperventilate back into a very light sleep. On the last visit, one of the resident doctors finally provided me with some insight into what was going on in the background:

1. *The thoracic surgeon felt that the biopsy could be handled differently and that slicing open my neck was a little extreme and a last-case scenario. He suggested that the procedure be done via a CT*

*scan guided biopsy. (I'll get into this procedure
with you later.)*

2. *The doctor from Radiology had no interest in
    or time for doing a CT scan guided biopsy and
    thought the best way to deal with my dilemma
    was to follow the original plan and slice away.*

This apparently would go on all night between the two sections of
the hospital and all I wanted was to just go home.

At around 6:30 in the morning my partner arrived to check in
on me and make sure that I hadn't broken out of the joint while
everyone slept. I think she was happy to see that I was still around
and hadn't had a *Prison Break* moment during the night.

I gave her all the wonderful details of my night and was happy
that she brought me some fresh clothing and reading material to
help pass the time. We waited around for a bit, and at approximately 7:15 a.m. I finally got the opportunity to meet with the
thoracic surgeon. He showed up with some of the residents who
had seen me during the night and explained the situation to my
partner and me in great detail, which we truly appreciated. We
discussed the procedure that was originally on the table and that
during the night they had spent a great deal of time fighting with
Radiology to push for a CT scan guided biopsy instead. They had
agreed that they were no longer going to slice me open—halle-
lujah!—but I would have to be admitted to the hospital for the
weekend for Radiology to agree to perform the procedure on that
Monday morning. (Sweet Jebus, if this was all I would have to do
for them not to open me up I would've signed on hours ago!)

Now, I've stated before that with every dark cloud there is a silver
lining and this was no exception. We talked about the logistics
and timing of the procedure and this wonderful man said the
magic words I wanted to hear.

I would be able to go home during the day, but I'd have to sleep at the hospital. Tears rolled down my face, my heart skipped a beat or two and I was filled with so much joy that it was hard to contain.

This dark cloud had more of a copper than a silver lining but, who cares, I was taking it.

I'm pretty sure I hugged this guy and thanked him profusely for not wanting to slice me open and allowing me to go home. We stayed at the hospital until they shipped me to my new room (I got a room and roommate) and after they checked my vitals and took some more blood I was now able to check myself out on a day pass. I would have to return by no later than 7:00 p.m. (an entire seven hours outside of that place)!

The rest of the day was a blur. And, just like a yo-yo, this story was in its upswing. Unfortunately, we were soon headed DOWN...but for now it was a small victory that I gladly relished.

TURN 10
THE GOOD, THE BAD AND THE MOANING

It amazes me how the body reacts to certain situations. I had spent the last couple of days hyperventilating and coming undone. Then four little words changed everything:

"YOU CAN GO HOME"

I fully understood that my elation about going home was to be short-lived as I would have to go back to the hospital within a few hours, but I'm still (even today) surprised at how much those words changed my outlook and feelings on the whole situation.

It was a warm, beautiful Saturday afternoon and while I wouldn't be able to ride my motorcycle due to the blood thinners, I didn't have to be stuck in a room waiting for the inevitable to happen.

On the bright side, my roommate seemed really nice and helped put things into perspective for me when I saw what he was dealing with. He had ripped the lining in his lung and had to have a weave mesh put in to ensure that his lung didn't collapse. The worst part of the whole thing was that he was attached to some sort of fluid removal machine and, yes, it was as gross as it sounds. He was pretty chill and good company during our time together. We laughed, cracked jokes about life and our ongoing issues, discussed the fact that he was still smoking even in this condition, etc. The night went by somewhat smoothly—that is, until the vampire nurse arrived to once again withdraw another vial of blood from my now bruised hand, arm, or anywhere else she could find a vein.

I was able to scare her with a heart rate of 220 and she exclaimed, "My goodness, are you okay?"

I assured her I was fine but that I'd be much better if she would just let the blood stay where it was meant to be—IN MY BODY—and stop trying to bleed me dry. We danced the usual waltz of "Let's Find a Vein in V Minor" and then I hyperventilated my way back to dreamland.

The next morning I arose to the sun coming through the window and got the fuck outta Dodge as quickly as I could. Little did I know that my roommate would be leaving during the day. When I returned at the required 7:00 p.m. cut-off, he was gone like the wind. Oh well, a room all to myself was fine, too (HA! My luck was not that good). At some point between my arrival and lights out, a new roommate arrived, and this would turn out to be the worst night I had had in the hospital yet.

I've been told that usually they don't put men and women together as roommates in hospitals but of course I would be the "lucky" one. I wasn't overly surprised when I saw that my new roommate was a woman in her late forties who was clearly in a lot of pain. I'm not sure what had happened to her but she spent—I'm not kidding—the entire night in obvious pain, moaning and groaning and calling for the nurse every twenty minutes or so.

My internal conversation went something like this:

"Breathe…stay calm… Head phones would be nice right about now… PLEASE LADY, SHUT THE FUCK UP!"

I realize that it may seem insensitive of me to have been thinking this way, but when you're dealing with your own little crisis every moment of sanity helps, and the sounds coming from the bed next to mine were not helping matters. To be honest, I don't recall much about that night other than toying with the idea of smothering the lady with a pillow so that I could focus on my gasping for air.

Serenity Now… Insanity Later!

TURN 11
MONDAY, MONDAY

Ahhhhh...a lazy Monday morning...the birds chirping...the sun shining and...

"Nurse!"

OH, FOR FUCK'S SAKE! (For a split second you thought the story had changed, didn't you? Well, not so much.)

The day of reckoning was finally here. It was around 6:30 a.m. and I hadn't really slept much during the night because of someone's constant calling for the nurse. My nerves were shot and were starting to get the better of me. At around 6:45 a.m. the nurse came in to remove one more vial of blood and provide me with one last dose of blood thinners (the last that would be administered to me by a nurse for the next ten months; from then on it was all up to me). Once the orderly showed up it would be off to the biopsy we'd go. In the meantime, my partner arrived to see me sitting in a chair staring off into oblivion.

"What are you doing sitting there?" she asked.

"Nothing, just trying not to kill anyone and breathing," I replied.

She could see in my face that I hadn't slept well. Most of the night had been spent curled up in a ball with a pillow over my head trying to drown out the unpleasant sounds of my roommate. I was nervous, agitated and tired, but at least this would bring some clarity to my situation and we would now be able to deal with the C-Beast head-on.

The orderly arrived and advised that it was time to go to Radiology. I got up, grabbed my IV machine and started walking out the door when I was told that I had to hop on the gurney and they would push me. WAIT, WHAT?...I can walk!

For some reason that I have yet to understand I was not allowed to walk myself. Instead I had to lie down and be wheeled there on a bed. I begrudgingly accepted this and away we went down to Radiology, through the hallways, in and out of the elevator and into the waiting area. The closer we got to the eleventh hour, the more my breathing changed from semi-calm to distressed. The doctor arrived with her clipboard and pen in hand and proceeded to ramble on about what they were going to do. She then handed me the pen and clipboard and requested that I sign a release waiver...just in case there were any complications or they accidentally killed me during the biopsy.

Now it was time to PANIC! PANIC!! PANIC!!!

I asked the doctor if there was any possibility of getting something to calm me down and she said that she'd get the nurse to bring me an Ativan before we began the procedure. In the meantime we just waited around. At some point the nurse arrived and checked my IV line to make sure everything was flowing but, as I looked around, there didn't seem to be any magic pills in her hand. She smiled and said it would be another ten to fifteen minutes before I'd be up to bat and then began walking away.

Hey, wait a minute...come back here...you forgot...

Panic set in once again.

TURN 12
SHOT TO THE HEART (PART I)

I feel I should probably provide some context as to what was actually going on inside of me before I continue with this story...

WARNING: What comes next might be considered some scary shit and may freak some of you out, but fear not my friends, I'm much better now. Ready?

My CT scan showed the following:

- I had a mass in my chest that was approximately six centimetres long by five centimetres wide and was cupping my heart while slowly suffocating it.

- I had a swollen lymph node in my left arm that had caused the blood clot as it was pushing on my brachial vein, which slowed the blood flow down.

- I had the beginning signs of a swollen lymph node appearing in my diaphragm.

- Last but not least, there was a lymph node that was pushing on my larynx, which explained why I was having a hard time speaking for extended periods and felt nauseated.

In case you need a visual explanation of what was going on inside my body, imagine a nuclear explosion and the fallout that comes with it. (For the record, humour is by far the best medicine.)

Now that you know what was happening inside me, where was I?

The nurse came by and left but hadn't provided me with the requested Ativan and we were T-minus-holy-shit minutes to lift-off. The thought of standing on the gurney and having a temper tantrum crossed my mind but my partner got the nurse's attention and she requested the Ativan once again, and this time the nurse obliged with not one but two wonderful little pills.

Phew! That was close...

"Okay, sir, we're going to take you in now," the orderly said and they pushed me into the CT scan room.

The cool part of this whole thing was that the technicians were the same group of people I had met a few days earlier and they were extremely friendly and helpful, even though I'm sure I was a complete mess. They plugged me into the machine and I was told over the speaker to follow the instructions, relax and breathe normally like I had during the last CT scan. Once I entered the Circle of Death and returned, the next step was to have me remove my gown so that they could disinfect and mark my chest. After which the doctor would arrive and administer the local anesthetic, which would of course consist of another god-damn needle...

Will this needle finally burst our hero's bubble?

Tune in next time to find out, same 6ix-day, same 6ix-channel…

TURN 13
SHOT TO THE HEART (PART II)

Last week when we left our "hero" we were...

Ah, yes. Needles, probes and the Circle of Death (CT scanning machine)...

The doctor proceeded to make a small incision on the marked area of my chest and inserted what I can only describe as the largest, thickest and widest needle I have ever seen in my life, and I now had this metal rod sticking six to eight inches out of my chest. For a brief moment I felt as if I was in a horror movie. On any normal day this most definitely would've freaked me out but today was not a normal day and, thanks to those magic little pills I had been given earlier, I was as cool as a cucumber. Everyone cleared the room and once again I was going to be put back into the Circle of Death for scanning.

While I lay there waiting and trying not to freak out, I looked at this thing sticking out of me and began to wonder if there was enough clearance to go back into the machine without incident. Oh well, only time would tell. Back in I went (incident-free) and once again was to follow the instructions I was given over the loudspeaker and relax.

Breathe in…now hold…breathe out…and repeat.

Out of the machine I came and the doctor and nurse returned to continue with this twisted scene of carnage. The doctor grabbed a probe that looked like a longer, thinner version of a needle with fingers on the end of it. This was going to be inserted through the needle that was already in my chest to remove a few samples. Every couple of seconds I heard a clicking sound and the doctor would remove what I assumed to be another sample and place it on a tray and then go back in for more. This happened about fourteen or fifteen times—which was way more than a few—and all the while she kept asking me if I was okay and if I was feeling any pain or discomfort. (How does one even respond to that when you've got a metal pole sticking out of your chest?)

A few minutes of sample removal passed and the doctor finally removed the probe for the last time, pulled out the guiding tube from my chest, placed a Band-Aid over the incision she had originally made and we were done. They unplugged me from the Circle of Death, cleaned me up and wheeled me out no worse for wear. This was way more effective than putting me under, slicing open my neck and getting those samples as they had originally wanted to do! The doctor then told me that I would need to stay in the waiting area for approximately an hour to ensure that they hadn't punctured my lung or done anything else that could cause a complication and that I would require an X-ray to confirm.

A PUNCTURED LUNG? A COMPLICATION? WHAT THE HELL DID THEY DO IN THERE?

We hung around the waiting area and I lay there and watched my heart rate on the monitor while the effects of both the pills and anesthetic slowly faded away. I wasn't in a great amount of pain or discomfort, but with every breath it was pretty obvious that something had been inside my chest. They called me over to do the X-ray and once it was complete and they saw that they hadn't punctured anything, I was again transported to my room where I could pack up and finally go home.

I arrived at my room and to my surprise and delight there was no roommate in sight and it was, for once, quiet on the floor. I wondered what had happened to my roommate while I was getting dressed and packing up but was glad for the moment of solitude and serenity while I got ready to leave. I signed a few forms, thanked everyone for putting up with me and was now...

FREE AS A BIRD – The Beatles

TURN 14
IT'S ALL ABOUT THE MUSIC

"And the Death card doesn't mean you die
It means a change is coming that you simply can't deny.
Reborn! Rebirth!"
– Machine Head

It's time for a musical interlude. July 18 will forever be a special day for me as it marks the anniversary of my diagnosis. I thought I'd share with you some of the uplifting tunes that helped me get through this tumultuous journey. There were many songs that had a great impact on me and changed both my views on life and the way I see things from a day-to-day perspective. These songs are from various genres and eras. Below is a playlist from my iPod of the songs that helped me get through this mess:

- "Just Breathe" – Pearl Jam

- "Wasted Words" – As I Lay Dying

- "À Tout le Monde" – Megadeth

- "It's Probably Me" – Sting

- "Albatross" – Big Wreck

- "Wiser Time" – The Black Crowes

- "Who Wants to Live Forever" – Queen

- "Time" – Big Wreck

- "Weak Willed " – All That Remains

- "Killers & Kings" – Machine Head

- "Soul Breaking" – The Tea Party

- "Metalingus" – Alter Bridge

- "Control" – Big Wreck

- "The Grand Optimist" – City and Colour

- "Seven Bridges Road" – Eagles

- "Can't Trust It" – Public Enemy

- "Good Riddance" – Green Day

- "Radioactive" – Imagine Dragons

- "Timeshel" – Mumford & Sons

- "No More Tears" – Ozzy Osbourne

- "Do the Evolution" – Pearl Jam

- "Under the Bridge" – Red Hot Chili Peppers

- "Back to the Moment" – Slash's Snakepit

- "From Can to Can't" – Corey Taylor and Dave Grohl

- "Epiphany" – Staind

- "Through Glass" – Stone Sour

- "Too Numb to Cry " – Zakk Wylde

- "Come Undone" – Duran Duran

- "Yesterday Don't Mean Shit" – Pantera

- "Grace" – Lam of God

- "The Dolphin's Cry" – Live

- "Big City Lights" – Black Stone Cherry

- "Spiral" – Godsmack

- "Learn to Fly" – Foo Fighters

- "Reunion" – Collective Soul

- "All In" – Lifehouse

- "Spoke in the Wheel" – Black Label Society

- "All My Life" – Foo Fighters

- "Santeria" – Sublime

- "'Til We Die" – Slipknot

- "Little Black Submarines" – The Black Keys

- "Behind Blue Eyes" – Limp Bizkit

- "I've Got You Under My Skin" – Frank Sinatra

- "My Morning Song" – The Black Crowes

- "Change (In the House of Flies)" – Deftones

- "Fuck Your Enemy" – Superjoint Ritual

- "Whispers" – All That Remains

- "Stairway to Heaven" – Led Zeppelin

- "Combustion" – Meshuggah

- "Easy" – Faith No More

- "You Are Not Alone" – Desolate Rage (to be explained later)

While you're listening to these tunes, here's a list of a few sites that you are welcome to check out to get some insight into what Hodgkin Lymphoma is all about:

Lymphoma Canada – www.lymphoma.ca

Lymphoma Research Foundation – www.lymphoma.org

Lymphoma Coalition – www.lymphomacoalition.org

Partnership Against Cancer – www.Partnershipagainstcancer.ca

Know Your Nodes – www.lymphoma.ca/know-your-nodes

TURN 15
WHAT NEXT?

Ahhhh, home sweet hell. I was to have a day or two to relax in between tests but it quickly became clear that there wouldn't be much of that going on as I still had to contend with work, my heightened anxiety, the acceptance of all that was happening and two—yes, that's right folks—TWO daily needles that I would need to inject myself with to keep my blood good and thin.

Note: These injections would be the daily regimen for approximately nine months and there are some rather interesting side effects that can occur, such as:

- Unusual bleeding (nose, mouth, etc.)

- General bruising, purple or red pinpoint spots under the skin

- Feeling light-headed or short of breath, rapid heart rate, trouble concentrating

- Bloody stools, coughing up blood, or vomit that looks like coffee grounds

- Pain, irritation, redness, or swelling where the medicine was injected

- Fever

- Nausea, diarrhea

- Pain or burning while urinating

- Fast or irregular heartbeat

The days went by in a flash. I would have these weird fits of crying and/or rage and then just as quickly shut it down and be normal again. This couldn't have been healthy for anyone around me and I'm sure it was very confusing as it seemed to happen out of the blue. I'd be in the car listening to music, driving somewhere, and would have to pull over to deal with the tears, or be in the kitchen and look at something random in the fridge and break down. Every/any little thing could set off a nuclear meltdown.

On Tuesday we were back at the hospital and I had the pleasure of meeting my "real" oncologist this time and unlike my first interaction with an oncologist, this one was much better. We waited in the office and in came the doctor and right off the bat he seemed to understand the fragility of the situation and gingerly (so as to not upset the beast) explained what the plan was going to be and where we were headed. This was great! We now had a plan of attack and would know soon enough what the deal was. I recall him saying,

"If you wanted cancer—"

"I didn't, but I'll play along," I interrupted.

"—this was the one to get," he continued.

There were going to be a couple of steps that I would have to take before we were to start chemo, and over the next couple of days I'd be back at the hospital to complete the following:

- Step 1: CT scan guided biopsy and samples to be removed and sent to the lab for testing. (Done and done!)

- Step 2: A gallium scan (full-body radioactive test) to see every slice of me from top to bottom.

- Step 3: A bone marrow biopsy to ensure everything was copacetic in the blood and bones. (This would be a fun one.)

We were finished with the first step of this process. They had removed whatever samples they needed and were going to analyse them and return the results in a few days. (SWEET!) The next few steps and days were going to be interesting ones.

TURN 16
I'M RADIOACTIVE

"I'm waking up, I feel it in my bones
Enough to make my system blow
Welcome to the new age, to the new age
I'm radioactive, radioactive"
– Imagine Dragons

I awoke Wednesday morning with this feeling of calm and relief as if the last couple of days had been a bad dream and everything was now okay. I was quickly reminded by the blood thinners I injected myself with that this was just the beginning of my journey and we were headed down a turbulent path.

I was off to work to explain to my peeps what was going on and speak to my director about what was in store over the next few days and onward, as I would need to be at the hospital again later on that afternoon to complete another test. We decided that I would spend the next few days dealing with the medical side of things and he wanted my partner and me to come into the office and speak with him after the weekend, but that I should focus on staying positive and getting better.

Back to the hospital we went for Step Two. This was to be one of the most interesting tests I would do during my first couple of days on this journey. A gallium scan is what was on tap at the Nuclear Medicine ward of the hospital. The fact that there was an area of the hospital called Nuclear Medicine should have been an omen of what was to come next, but it didn't really hit home until I got there. Let me set the scene for you:

- There are radioactive signs everywhere.

- Medicine and dyes are transported in lead cases.

- There is a separate bathroom strictly for patients' use.

- It is relatively dark and there are no windows of any kind.

I met with the nurse and provided him with the requisition I was given by my oncologist.

"Okay, great. Have you had anything to drink this morning?" he pleasantly asked.

"Some water and a coffee," I replied.

"Please ensure that you use the bathroom and then head over to that chair. I'll come over shortly and we'll get you all set up."

I really didn't have to use the facilities but gave it the old college try and then headed over to the chair that he had directed me to.

The nurse showed up with his crash cart and a small lead box with radioactive logos on it.

Once again we danced the forbidden dance of "Let's Find a Vein" and after it was flushed and ready for yet another fluid to be injected into me, the nurse opened the lead box. Inside sat a syringe (of course) filled with a neon green fluid. It was also encased in lead with a small viewer to see inside. I began having these weird visions of turning into a glowing green Mr. Burns from *The Simpsons*.

He injected me with the radioactive shit and advised that I'd have to wait for approximately thirty minutes before we could begin the test. He also mentioned that I was to stay put, and if I required the bathroom that I use the one designated for patients and no other. (Now why would that be?)

The nurse returned as promised about thirty minutes later and escorted me over to a dark room with a metal table and what I can only describe as a massive camera hanging above it. I was to lie on my back on the table and not move for the next ninety minutes while this monstrosity of a camera would hover over my body and do its thing. I tried to stay calm and focused on breathing at a normal pace and slowly drifted off into dreamland during the test. Ninety minutes went by in a blink and we were now done with Step Two. The nurse came back, escorted me to the chair and removed the IV line from my hand. I was free! As I was getting ready to leave he said,

"So, for the next twenty-four hours, if you could, please do not use the same bathroom as anyone else in your home."

COME AGAIN...WHAT???

TURN 17
HAPPY BIRTHDAY

HAPPY BIRTHDAY TO ME, HAPPY BIRTHDAY TO ME, HAPPY BIRTHDAY DEAR SELFIE... Oops! Wrong singalong.

(I have to admit it's a pretty awesome gift that I'm still able to celebrate another year of being alive.)

Thursday morning was here and I was back at the hospital again meeting with my oncologist. We discussed the results of my biopsy and what the gallium scan had confirmed, and all signs were pointing in the same direction:

STAGE THREE, CLASSIC HODGKIN LYMPHOMA WITH NODULAR SCLEROSIS.

It was pretty clear what the plan was going to be and it was just a matter of time before we started my chemo treatments. My oncologist explained the treatment plan and some possible short/long-term side effects of the ABVD chemo treatment (AWESOME!) and they were as follows:

- Low number of blood cells

- Feeling and being sick post treatment

- Diarrhea and constipation during treatment cycles

- A sore mouth and mouth ulcers

- Hair loss or thinning (I'll get into to that one shortly)

- Feeling tired and run down

- Extreme body pain

- Infertility (It was time to freeze the boys or girls)

- Heart disease

- Lung damage

But, before we could begin, there was still a matter of this bone marrow biopsy that had to be completed in the following week and, assuming it was clear, we would begin the first round of planned chemo therapy on August 8. We verbally jousted about working during treatment and decided we would take it on a week-by-week basis, but for now I would work and go through chemo at the same time (to some people's dismay).

Looking back, this idea of working and chemo-ing was probably not the smartest move in the world, but I needed some sort of normalcy in my life as things were slowly being taken away from me bit by bit (i.e. motorcycle, hockey, softball, playing live, etc.).

Now, about this hair loss thing, there was no way in hell that I was going to lose my hair because of treatment. On that Friday I went into work and, during the morning, waffled back and forth about what to do. I decided that it would be a wonderful time to convert my long hair into a Mohawk. At lunch I walked to the hairdresser, sat in the chair and…

"What would you like to do today?" she asked.

"I'd like a Mohawk, please," I replied.

"Why?" she asked.

"Because I have cancer and I'm not going to lose my hair on anyone else's terms!"

Once again I may have been a little snappy and a person who had nothing to do with my situation got to feel my wrath. I apologized profusely after my little outburst and we planned the attack on my head, and the hairdresser ensured me that my hair would get donated as requested.

TURN 18
THE REVEAL AND PLAN

Friday evening my mother was due to return from overseas and we would have to bring her up to speed on what had transpired over the last little while, as she was out of the loop by design. (Ugh, not a fun conversation.) I was also now ready to let my friends know what was going on as I hadn't seen most of them since I had been spending copious amount of time lately at the hospital doing all those tests, and I was sure they were starting to figure out that something wasn't right.

We met with my mother for dinner and broke the news to her. She was surprisingly calm about the whole situation and, to be honest, having her freak out at this point wouldn't have done anyone any good. Looking back, in retrospect it was the best possible reaction given the news and the situation at hand (although she said, as most mothers do, that she had some idea there was something wrong). Later that evening my partner and I met up with my friends to give them the news and bring them up to speed, as well. They were similarly calm but I could tell that they, too, were concerned and while I was trying to keep a strong face they could see that I was scared shitless about what was coming and what the future held in store. We all hung out and had a good laugh about my new hairdo and this seemed to ease the mood a little.

(Looking back I can't even imagine what was running through their heads, and during this entire process they were fantastic. Strong, supportive and uplifting, they were never short on jokes, always there to lend an ear when I needed to vent and offered as much love, care and positive vibes as they could to help me get through it. I will forever be in their debt.)

My partner's parents came and visited us that weekend, as well, and we had a birthday dinner for me on the Saturday with my parental units, my partner's parents and my brother. It was a wonderful evening of all-you-can-eat-sushi and Thai cuisine at Spoon & Fork where everyone ate, drank and celebrated my thirty-fifth birthday (or as I called it then, my last supper). There was a heightened sense of anxiety during the evening, but we were making the best of my situation, all things considered. I'm forever grateful for having us all together, but I will never be able to shake that sense of anxiety whenever my birthday comes around.

The next step would be to go into work to discuss an action plan for the foreseeable future and complete my final test, a bone marrow biopsy, before we were off to the races with chemo.

TURN 19
IT'S LIKE REAL 3D

Loaded with a ton of information, I connected with work and my partner and I went in and met with my office director and explained my situation. I have to say that everyone at work was incredibly supportive and together we drafted a plan that would be suitable for everyone and would grant me the flexibility to work and do chemo without any issues. My partner and director came to an agreement that if I was at work and I looked—or someone felt I looked—sick, that I would be sent home and we would reassess accordingly, but for now it would be three quarter days for me and I'd work from home if and when possible.

It was Tuesday morning and the day of reckoning was finally here… It was Bone Marrow Biopsy Day (and you thought it was Chemo Day). We arrived at the hospital and made our way into the oncologist's office and a wonderful nurse was present and administered the following:

- Four milligrams of morphine (that shit burns when it's being injected)

- Two Gravol (just in case I felt queasy)

- Two Ativan (for good measure and to keep me calm)

I'd like to point out that this little cocktail has some serious effects on a person and causes some short-term memory loss, so what happened over the next several minutes is based on third-party accounts. Over time, the memories started coming back to me but it took about three to four weeks and some things were just always blurry.

There I was, sitting on the edge of the gurney, rocking back and forth, while my partner and father sat in front of me. I vaguely recall my partner suggesting that I lie down and wait for the doctor to arrive. I harshly responded with a "No! I'm fine here." She smiled and shrugged her shoulders and let me continue on rocking away. At one point I recall saying, "This is like real 3D. I see you, the chair, the wall, the wall, the chair and then you."

My partner just looked at me and laughed along with my father and so long as I didn't smash my face on the ground from falling off the gurney there really wasn't any harm being done. Shortly after this one-sided conversation, I pleasantly had another similar conversation with my nurse. She asked me to lie down and I also proceeded to tell her that I wanted to wait for the doctor to arrive before I lay down. She also shrugged her shoulders and let me be. (Little did I know that she would play a prominent role during my treatment and my recollection of her would be a foggy one to start.)

My doctor arrived and my partner and father left the room. Once they closed the door to the office, he advised I would have to take off my pants for the procedure and lie on my stomach. According to someone (my nurse) I proceeded to tell my oncologist that I could remove my pants without unbuttoning them and then willingly pantsed myself, jumped up on the gurney and got ready for the procedure (not my proudest moment). I was administered a local anesthetic on my hip and off we went. I don't recall much except being told at one point that what was going to happen next would be the most pain I would ever feel in my entire life, but it would be over quickly. Hmmmm…I thought. I wonder what…

HOLY FUUUUUUUUUUUUUCKKKKKKKKKING SHIT!!!!!

Turns out that the local anesthetic for this procedure is simply to numb the pain from the corkscrew that is inserted into your hip, and it will not numb the pain of bone marrow being extracted from your body.

Once the procedure was over, I vaguely recall my doctor telling me that I could put my pants on and that based on the difficulty he had removing my bone marrow, the chances of anything being wrong in my bones were slim. He was sweating like a madman and sounded out of breath and it would explain a great deal of what was going on during the procedure, as it felt like someone was pushing on my hip the whole time.

TURN 20
RETURN OF THE PEACOCK SHOOTER

*(Think of a peacock combined with Shooter
McGavin from Happy Gilmore)*

If you've gone this far, congrats! You've travelled through most of
these twists and turns and hopefully have gotten a sense of what
this journey was like. You've read a little about my family and the
people in my life at the time and have probably gotten a sense of
the type of person that I am, as well.

Shall we continue?

Okay...

The procedure was complete and I was as high as a kite. It was now
time to find my dad and partner and head on out of the hospital.

My partner came back into the doctor's office and had a good laugh seeing me trying to put my pants back on, as apparently taking them off was much easier than putting them back on. I got my shit together, threw on my sunglasses (because everyone needs to wear sunglasses inside) and was ready to go. I stumbled out of the oncologist's office and started making my way to the nurse's desk. My partner tried to hold my hand while we were walking, but I apparently would have none of it. (She was walking and I was making a valiant effort at it, but it was more like swerving).

"Hold my hand," she said.

"No," I responded like a child.

I somehow made my way to the counter without incident, whipped off my sunglasses and sputtered,

"Ladies, is there anything that I need from you or you need from me before I go?" I asked.

"No, just head on home and get some rest," they said with a smile and a laugh.

"OOOOOO-KAAAAY," I responded as I started strolling away.

My father watched this train wreck and of course had a great laugh while he walked away and my partner eyeballed me with a look that said, "Dude, really? I'm standing right here beside you."

"Wait! I need to renew the plate sticker for the car and motorcycle!" I exclaimed.

Once again I received another "Dude, really?" look and was told that if I wanted to go renew the sticker for the car and motorcycle that my dad would have to take me as she (my partner) had no interest in going with me to the Ministry of Transportation Office. My dad chuckled about the whole thing and agreed to take me. So off we went to the MTO to renew the stickers for both the car and motorcycle.

We headed to the MTO and I was able to renew the stickers for both car and bike and then I headed home for some much needed rest. This was it—a few more days and we'd be hauling the mail and starting chemo. The closer we got to the date the more nervous I became and, to top it off, there were still a few last-minute housekeeping items that needed to be sorted out before we got this party started.

(A quick tidbit of advice for all of you: Do not under any circumstances try to do anything after a bone marrow biopsy, as the drugs administered to you will make it extremely difficult to do anything post-surgery.)

TURN 21
ROUND EIGHT (ROPE-A-DOPE)

"I love the smell of chemo in the morning"
– The Bucket List (2007)

This was it. This was what the last two-and-a-half weeks of X-rays, Ativan, blood removal, panic attacks, blood thinners, CT scans, biopsies and profanity had been leading up to. It was early Wednesday morning on August 8, 2012, and I lifted my head from the pillow and prepared myself for what would be the first of many bi-weekly visits to the hospital for a little chemotherapy over the next nine to ten months.

I was thirty-five and was being forced to accept the fact that I was no longer as invincible as I had believed. I went downstairs and drank what would be my last cup of coffee for the next nine or ten months (the chemo would make my taste buds despise the sweet nectar of the gods) and, as always, thinned out my blood with my prescribed Lovenox. We hopped in the car and made our way to the hospital and arrived earlier than expected, which, of course, gave me time for a little freak-out session.

I arrived at the nurses' station, joked around for a bit with the staff, presented my health card and was then handed a clipboard, asked to fill out a form, return it once completed and told to grab a number. They would call my number shortly so that they could remove some of my now-thinner, precious blood. I paced around in the waiting area until I heard...

"Number three, number three!" the nurse called out.

"That's me," I responded.

"Come with me, please."

Away we went into a little room just across the hall from the waiting area and I was directed to sit down and roll up my sleeve. The nurse was fantastic. She was gentle and very quickly understood, based on the look on my face, that this was not my most favorite thing in the world to be doing. She calmly walked me through what was going to happen and we spoke about the possibility of removing my precious blood from my hand instead of my arm as I was still nervous about going after a vein up there due to the blood clot.

She indulged me and quickly and painlessly removed the blood she needed and I was done. It was by far the easiest blood removal since I had started this little hospital journey. I'd see her every two weeks going forward and it was always a pleasant and pain-free visit (and Lord knows how much I hate needles).

Once we were done with blood removal, I filled out the information on the clipboard and the next thing I knew I was being called again by another nurse who looked vaguely familiar. It would take a couple of weeks but I would slowly recall with some help who this foggy lady was and why she looked so familiar. You'd think that after sharing a dreamy pantsing of oneself in front of her I'd have fond memories of who she was but apparently not. We walked over to a scale where she weighed me, checked my heart rate, verified my height, and confirmed that I was not on any type of medication other than the blood thinners.

We were done with the pre-chemo assessments…this was it…I was now officially in the hands of the doctors and nurses and no longer had control over the situation. As I briefly mentioned before, my chemo treatment would be every two weeks and the routine would be the same for the next nine or ten months. It would look a little something like this:

08:15 - Arrive at the hospital and nervously pace around

08:30 - Fill out clipboard form, get blood taken and weigh in

09:00 - Two Stemetil pills to help with possible nausea and three dexamethasone pills

- CAUSE A RUCKUS -

09:15-09:30 – 250 ml of saline solution to flush everything at the start

10:00-11:00 - Three chemos to be pushed

A – Doxorubicin (Adriamycin)

B – Bleomycin

V – Vinblastine

- BIO BREAK & CAUSE ANOTHER RUCKUS –

11:15-11:30 - Another 250 ml of saline solution to flush everything again

11:45-13:45 - One chemo mixed in a 1000 ml drip bag

D – Dacarbazine (DTIC)

13:45-14:00 – 250 ml of saline solution as a final flush

*Approx. 14:15 - Released from my prison and
out into the real world for two weeks*

The staff was supportive and they put up with all of my shit disturbing and would make my days there fun and bring some light-heartedness and levity to a very serious and heavy situation. While the routine sounds bad it became one that I would make the best of over the next while. What I wasn't prepared for was what I was to experience a few days later, as the drugs would leave my system…

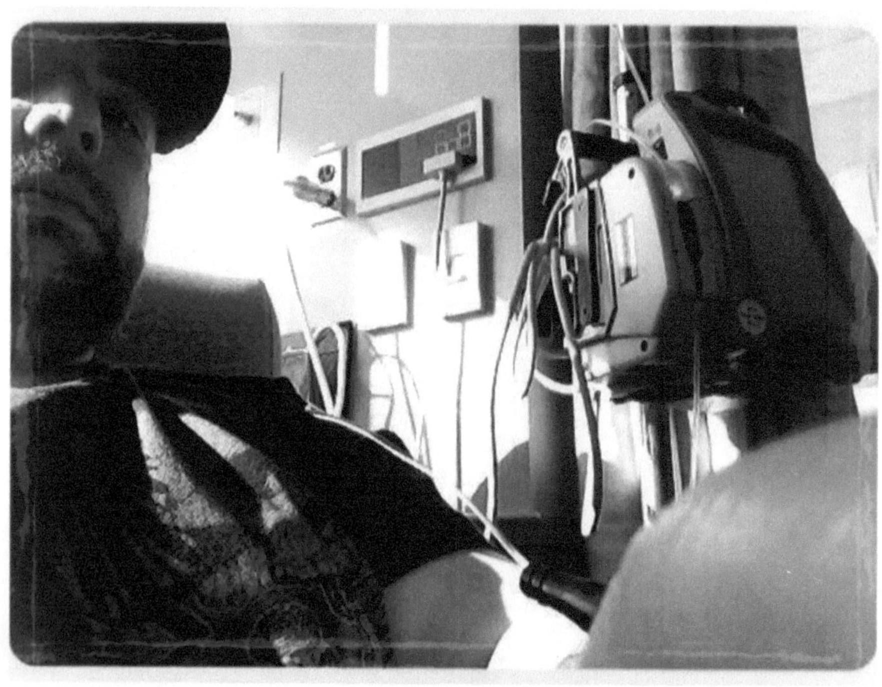

TURN 22
THE MAC TRUCK EFFECT

Chemotherapy is not a one-size-fits-all experience. It can be draining, both physically and mentally, and every patient describes their experiences with chemotherapy differently. Some may have stomach cramps and diarrhea for the duration of the treatment. Others suffer very bad side effects such as mouth ulcers, constant vomiting, joint pain and hair loss, and then there are the people who say they felt no side effects from the treatment at all. The symptoms vary from patient to patient and I wasn't sure what lucky number I had drawn but I would soon find out.

I finished with the first of what would become my usual Wednesday treatments around 2:00 p.m. and we headed over to the pharmacy to pick up the remaining pills that I was required to take for the following three days (Stemetil and dexamethasone) and then headed home. For the next couple of days after chemo

I would feel fantastic (the steroids help with recovery) and while I'd look like Kermit the Frog's faded brother—I was a nice shade of pale green and yellow—I always felt pretty good physically and had a ton of energy, that is until the steroids would wear off.

It was very much the same routine for me after every single round of chemo and while it would get old very quickly, I was happy to know what was coming and it gave me time to prepare myself for the Monday-morning system failure I would endure. Saturday was the last day I would take the Dexamethasone and by Sunday night I'd begin to feel a few light aches and pains in my body. It was so routine, that on the few occasions I wouldn't feel any of the usual aches and pains, I would say to my partner,

"Maybe I won't feel any pain tomorrow and it'll be different."

"So hopeful," she'd respond.

We'd both laugh a little about it but I always knew she was right, and, while I would be hopeful, it was just delayed and the aches and pains were a comin'.

I have gone back and forth trying to think of a way to describe how I would feel on the Monday after chemo during those ten months. The closest I can come to describe it is that what is going on inside of you is at a cellular level and no amount of Advil, Tylenol or any other over-the-counter drug will dull the pain. In the movie *The Bucket List,* Morgan Freeman's character does a pretty good job of describing how it feels:

"...LIKE YOUR BONES ARE MADE OF NAPALM... IT'S A DAY AT THE BEACH."
— THE BUCKET LIST (2007)

Even now I still feel as though I can never truly explain this to anyone and when I try to explain it to someone I always just say that it felt like I was hit by a Mac truck. Holy shit...the body pains were insane and it would be a forty-eight-hour affair, me lying in bed trying to sleep it off and then coming downstairs and sitting on the couch trying to distract myself from the pain I would feel. It got so bad that later on in my treatment I decided to try a different method of pain management and I will say that the recommendation that I received was gladly appreciated and tasty, too. (The green brownies were so yummy and helpful and I would recommend this form of pain management to anyone who experienced the same thing I did).

Throughout all of this I have to say that I can't even begin to imagine how helpless my partner and the people around me felt as they watched me suffer. Again, I consider myself one of the lucky ones as my symptoms were limited to massive body pain and not your usual vomiting, diarrhea, etc.

TURN 23
THE KOREAN BBQ INCIDENT

Now that we've got the aches and pains out of the way, there are some interesting side effects of the post-chemo pills I was taking. More specifically, the dexamethasone.

Generic Name: Dexamethasone (oral) (dex-a-METH-a-sone)

What is dexamethasone?

Dexamethasone is a corticosteroid that prevents the release of substances in the body that cause inflammation. It is used to treat many different inflammatory conditions such as allergic disorders, skin conditions, ulcerative colitis, arthritis, lupus, psoriasis and breathing disorders.

So there you have it, dexamethasone is a steroid and with its use come some very interesting side effects...such as:

I would be a hungry, hungry hippo 24/7 while I was taking this little pill. The messed-up part is that no one told me this would be the case. Every symptom I was feeling was new to me and those around me, so we would deal with them on a case-by-case basis.

For five days after the chemotherapy, I could (and sometimes would) consume anything and everything in my sight and couldn't seem to ever fill the void in my stomach. As an example, breakfast would consist of a meal replacement shake, six Eggo waffles and fruit. It was crazy and inconceivable how hungry I was.

On a Thursday evening after my second or third round of chemo treatment, my partner and I made plans to go out for all-you-can-eat Korean BBQ and sushi with some of her colleagues, as they hadn't seen us since I started treatment and this would also be a nice distraction from the obvious dark cloud looming over our heads. We met everyone at their place of work and walked to the Korean Grill House. It was just past 7:00 p.m. and I was starting to get hangry (hungry and angry) as I hadn't eaten in a while—that is, about fifteen or twenty minutes. We were seated and within minutes the food was on its way out. Sushi rolls, barbecue spare ribs, beef, chicken, fish, more sushi rolls, etc. The more they brought out the more I would put on the grill, cook and then eat. It was a crazy sight to watch and at one point there was a stack of empty trays sitting beside me and I was still looking to order more sushi. It was a pleasant evening and we all seemed to have some fun and I know it was a needed distraction for us, considering what we were going through.

Every time I think about that evening I can't help but be reminded of the Monty Python skit from *The Meaning of Life*. Any more food that night would have caused an explosion, even a wafer-thin dinner mint.

At some point in the evening we finally finished eating (or more specifically I did), paid the bill and walked back to the car. I recall looking over at my partner and saying,

"I'm so full."

"That's because you ate about two pounds of chicken, beef and sushi," she replied

"So full…" I responded.

For some reason no one actually said anything to me about it during dinner but from what I was told (because I honestly don't recall) I was like a machine, and even the people at the restaurant were surprised at how much I packed away. You see, what they don't tell you is that one of the many side effects of dexamethasone is increased appetite. As I mentioned earlier, it turned my body into a bottomless pit for the first five days post chemo and during my weigh-in every two weeks before treatment the nurse would present me with the wonderful news that I'd gained weight. (YAY! I hadn't been looking forward to that.)

I was always under the impression that when people went through chemotherapy they lost weight, looked frail and malnourished, but let me tell you that is not always the case. In ten months I would gain approximately fifty-five pounds, which is what happens when you're working through three-thousand-plus calories a day and doing nothing. This, my friends, is just the tip of the iceberg when it comes to dexamethasone.

TURN 24
DIGGING FOR GOLD

Ah, dexamethasone...your wonderful side effects have left me with so many good stories. As I had alluded to before, this post-chemo drug is pretty crazy and I've heard some comedy/horror stories from people close to me about their family members' bouts with this drug's side effects. For instance, I recall someone telling me of an incident with a type of fruit being thrown around the house because it wasn't the one they had originally asked for. I've heard stories of people yelling at the top of their lungs for no reason other than the fact that they didn't get their requested ice cream in time. I'm sure by now you can guess, but one of the other fabulous side effects of taking dexamethasone is extreme shifts in mood, a kind of "roid rage," if you will.

During my ten months of treatment I became very aware of my body's reactions to the drugs I was taking and while at first I had no real idea what was going on, it became very clear that my friend, dexamethasone, was altering my moods in extreme ways. There would be moments at home that I would freak out and have a complete meltdown for no reason (usually due to the fact that there wasn't some type of food I wanted in the house). I'd be speaking with someone and have a bout of 'chemo brain' and then go off the handle because I couldn't recall what I was talking about. These became very frustrating situations for me.

One of the funniest/scariest moments was during the week of my second round of chemo. My partner and I decided to head on down to Best Buy across from Sherway Gardens to pick up a few things. (Looking back on it now, going there on a Saturday afternoon was probably not the smartest decision but, alas, you live and you learn.) For some this will come as no surprise, but I usually have great luck in finding parking spaces right by entrances. (My friends say I get "valet parking" anywhere I go.) We got to the parking lot, pulled up to the front of the store and as luck would have it, a gentleman in a faded gold Toyota Corolla had his reverse lights on. Sweet! I was going to get my valet parking after all. I pulled up to the spot and hit my signal to let every other parking vulture know that this was my kill. We waited and waited and waited and wait...

"WHAT THE FUCK, MAN!" I yelled in the car as if the man in his car could hear me.

"Holy shit, what happened?" my partner, now startled, asked.

"THIS ASSHOLE IS DIGGING FOR GOLD AND WON'T LEAVE THE SPOT!" I continued.

"What are you talking about?" she asked again.

"HE'S TRYING TO PERFORM A FRONTAL LOBOTOMY AND WON'T MOVE HIS FUCKING CAR!"

(I'D LIKE TO INFORM YOU THAT WE'VE OFFICIALLY REACHED DEFCON 1)

You see, this wonderful gentleman was picking his nose and I swear, even today as I write this, that I thought he was going to find something other than snot up there. When I was younger, if I got upset about something, my dad (in his usual comedic fashion) would grab his guitar and sing me a song that at this moment seemed rather fitting. It went a little something like this:

"It' S-not funny

It' S-not funny

What comes out of your nose when you're happy, honey.

Snot Funny"

"Are you okay? Are you hungry?" my partner asked.

"I don't know, maybe," I answered.

"Okay, you need to calm down. We'll go and get you something to eat and come back after," she said.

This, ladies and gentlemen, is about as bad as it got for me. From that moment on I would become more and more aware of how the little things would affect me and would (in most cases) try to keep my emotions in check.

DEXAMETHASONE, YOU'RE AN EVIL LITTLE PILL!

TURN 25
BACK AND FORTH AGAIN

Ten months sounds like a long time but when you're in the thick of things, let me tell you that it goes by in the blink of an eye. I had been beaten down physically, emotionally and psychologically but was still going strong and always tried to keep a positive outlook on things. At the end of October 2012 it was finally decided that it was probably in my best interest to stop working and truly focus on myself and getting better. I had missed a single treatment due to a low blood cell count and was now on the hook and being told that it was either time that I pull the plug on work or it would be done for me. Truth be told I was beginning to feel the effects of the chemotherapy on my body and, looking back, it was time to get some rest.

I took my final weeks of vacation and then went on short-term leave for the following sixteen weeks in hopes that I would be healthy enough to get back to work in the New Year. I said my goodbyes to everyone and promised that I would continue to email them (although the chemo brain would not always produce the sharpest thoughts) and keep them up to date on how I was progressing through treatment.

Sent: January, 18, 2013 12:42:06 p.m.

> *Happy New Year everyone,*
>
> *I just thought I'd drop you all a line and give you a quick update as to how I'm doing and where things are at. As per my last email I had three chemos left for January and things have been moving along as expected without any speed bumps. My oncologist has set up an appointment for a gallium, CT, and PET scan for the second week of February.*
>
> *Assuming things look good I should have two preventative chemos after the scans and I'm hoping to be back to work on a graduated basis by March (not going to lie...looking forward to getting back into the swing of things again).*
>
> *Miss you all and I'm doing well and looking forward to seeing you all soon.*
>
> *Stay well and healthy during this time of the season and I'll be in touch with any other updates.*
>
> *Cheers*

From then on it was all pretty much the same routine week in and week out. Treatment every second Wednesday, recovery after that, and the only constant extra-curricular in my life was band practice every Thursday. That was a non-negotiable for me and the guys in the band made it abundantly clear that if I was not feeling well that I should let them know and they would rehearse without me. (I don't fucking think so!)

As time went on I continued to see the physical impact that chemo was having on me. The veins in my hands were now turning a beautiful, dark shade of charcoal, the hair on my arms and legs was now non-existent, my eyebrows were thinning out, I hadn't shaved my face in months due to lack of hair growth, I had dark circles around my eyes, I was bloated and looked completely drained.

Closer to the end of chemo, my oncologist met with us and advised that things were progressing nicely and he was now ready to send me to Princess Margaret Hospital (PMH) to meet with the radiologist to find out if I would require radiation post chemotherapy. I got my appointment and it was time to make a new friend at PMH. This was my first visit to PMH and, let me tell you, I hoped that it would be my last.

Throughout my treatment I spent my time at St. Joseph's Hospital on the sixth floor in a small oncology ward. I knew everyone who worked there and the patients were always the same people week in and week out. I built relationships with these people and we were like a family. PMH is nothing like that! I liken it to being in a factory where everything and everyone is numbered and they're pushing them through as quickly as they can. It was truly a sobering moment when we arrived and I saw the massive number of people who were dealing with their own cancer journey.

I checked in and made my way to the waiting area to wait for the radiologist and, as always when nervous, I paced back and forth until we met with the doctor. He called us into his office and after checking me over and reviewing my chart, asked a few questions.

"Do you smoke?"

"Not anymore, I quit about a month before I was diagnosed," I replied.

"Do you plan on starting up again?" he asked.

"No, thank you, I'm good. Why?" I inquired.

"You shouldn't. This is a very serious situation, very serious," he said.

(No shit, Dr. Obvious!)

After our little back-and-forth he gave me the best news I could've asked for: NO RADIATION! He advised that based on how things were progressing and the fact that the mass had been in my chest, radiation would not be in my best interest as it would do more damage than good. It was a relief to hear and I was grateful that things were progressing nicely. I couldn't get out of there fast enough. My friends, this was a massive victory and all signs were pointing in the right direction. I was slowly but surely getting through this.

TURN 26
CAUSING A RUCKUS AND SURPRISES

It was pretty much the same humdrum from August through April. There were a few speed bumps along the way but nothing I would consider important enough to write home about. I would spend my time in the oncology ward being a pest to the staff and trying to bring smiles to the faces of the other patients around me. It wasn't meant to be disruptive but rather uplifting and, looking back, I know it was just my way of getting through this journey and the hours spent sitting in the same spot every two weeks. Sometimes it was difficult and the lack of energy would keep me at bay and I'd sleep my hours away; other times it was a show. This was my way of giving back, and the best feeling in the world was seeing those smiles.

I recall moments where I'd give my nurse a hard time about not getting the same treatment as other patients and getting ripped off in this oncology ward. She would give me a look and threaten to send me away but it was all in good fun (shit, at least I hope that's how it came across). I would also give my oncologist a hard time but I figured, considering the circumstances, it was okay and I remember him saying once that I looked and acted as if I was just there to get vitamins and then go home.

THOSE WERE SOME STRONG-ASS VITAMINS, DOC!

There were bittersweet moments throughout and I learned how to not dwell on the bad ones. I made a promise to myself that once I was finished with treatment I would always go back to the oncology ward and bring the staff gifts of appreciation. I see the staff as my guardian angels and I owe them and many others the world for giving me my life back. I have shown up unannounced around Christmas every year just to see them and I always have something for the staff. The head nurse will ask me what the hell I'm doing there with a concerned look on her face and will very quickly realize that my visit is a social one. I also had the pleasure of surprising my nurse at her retirement party. I became very close to her during my time there and it might have been because our first meeting was the day I pantsed myself in front of her and my oncologist, or just the simple fact that every two weeks she was the person to draw the lucky straw of getting me as her patient and having to put up with my shenanigans. For the record, she didn't retire because of me!

I will forever be grateful to all the staff in the Oncology ward at St Joseph's Hospital and while my journey had a happy ending, it doesn't always end that way. I know how strong these people are and they deserve to be recognized on a daily basis for the care they take with all their patients.

DESOLATE RAGE
EVOLUTION'S MISTAKE

TURN 27
EVOLUTION'S MISTAKE

During the months I was in treatment there was always one constant component of normalcy: the band. The guys were truly amazing and supportive. They always left the ball in my court when it came to rehearsals, which I appreciated. We made a conscious decision very early on that live shows would be off the table for the year, so it was time to retire CONDEMNED and rebrand ourselves. (A year off and a few other house-cleaning items will do that.) During our temporary hiatus from the metal world we spent time writing new material and worked on coming up with a new name.

Weeks were spent discussing various names between the four of us and it came down to two or three choices, and we ended up with DESOLATE RAGE. It was a surprisingly easy decision considering how opinionated we all are. Now the machine was

in motion with a new name, social media outlet, website (www.
desolaterage.com) and some new material to work with, but it
had been almost six years since we had released anything. All
signs were pointing to the band going into the recording studio
to work on a new album, once I was done treatment of course.

We planned out our attack and on April 19, 2013, Desolate
Rage officially came to life with an inaugural show at the Velvet
Underground. It was one day after my last chemo treatment and
while I'm sure people were concerned about my health and well-
being it seemed rather fitting that the one constant in my life over
the last nine months be the first thing I do after treatment. I was
still going to be on blood thinners for two more weeks and there
would be no motorcycle riding until at least May, and hockey
season wouldn't start again until September.

The show went off without a hitch and we ended the night with
"You Are Not Alone," one of the newer songs we had written
during our temporary hiatus. The song is all about my time in the
cancer prison and what I was feeling:

"I've created the legend in my head

We'll scatter all my ashes when I'm dead

I thought I was stronger, better and faster

But in the end I'm just a scared bastard

Flipped 180 on a dime

Turned upside down in time

Death was just a formality

It's my perception of reality

I spent my days thinking I was in full control

Another stupid fucker without a soul

Didn't matter what others had to say

'Cause when you're living a lie you live from day to day

So what have I learned? (What have I learned?)
And what will it take? (What will it take?)
What does it matter if I don't stop and appreciate?
Fuck NO!
A lesson cultured (Lesson cultured)
From the inside out (From the inside out)
A push of the needle, a life of sickness to figure it out
YOU…ARE NOT…ALONE… (x4)"

I was filled with so much emotion when introducing the song that my voice cracked and as the guitar sounds filled the venue, a tear rolled down my face and a huge weight was momentarily lifted off my shoulders. During those moments on stage I recognized that things were going to be okay and I was grateful for all I had gone through. It was an amazing night but there was still work to be done. We decided that we'd start recording in May and began the process of pre-production with our producer after that glorious concert. We spent the next two to three months locked away in a recording studio, working on the album. We all agreed on the album title and it seemed rather fitting considering everything that had transpired over that year off. We had evolved, rebranded; I had become a different person during treatment and came out the other side a better one. We were EVOLUTION'S MISTAKE.

(To hear the full story in our collective words, check out our YouTube channel https://www.youtube.com/user/DesolateRageBand where our podcast, "Rage-Cast," probably does a better job explaining it).

RUM FOR THE CURE
NIAGARA FALLS
EST. 2012

TURN 28
R.F.T.C. (RUM FOR THE CURE)

Once treatment was complete I felt as if my life never really went back to normal. It was now the new norm and I was learning to accept my new-found health and outlook on life. There were still tests to be done, blood to be given to anyone that wanted it and monthly check-ups with my oncologist to ensure that things were stable. I consider myself a very fortunate creature to have had so many people around me who cared. They were always there to lend an ear, be a support system and/or a safe space for me to have a momentary meltdown without judgment. I have a very close-knit group of friends that I consider more family than friends and they always seemed to know what to say or do to keep my spirits up throughout the entire process.

When the tests were complete and the proverbial dust settled, we decided that it would be a great time to head to Niagara Falls to celebrate my new-found health with a night of silliness and booze. Of course, trying to plan an event of this nature with more than one or two people is like herding cats. It is not an easy task, but we all managed to find a date that worked and off we went.

A night in Niagara Falls was exactly what the doctor ordered and it was laced with many laughs, tears, embraces and heartfelt moments between close friends (kind of like a Taster's Choice commercial). Two rooms, nine guys, a Boston Pizza and booze were on the menu. The evening would play out a little like this:

1. *Arrive in Niagara Falls and get settled in the hotel rooms.*

2. *Pre-drink in the designated drinking room for a bit and finish with a toast using home-made moonshine.*

3. *Walk to the Boston Pizza for dinner.*

4. *Back to the hotel to relax and drink some more.*

5. *Return to the Boston Pizza later that evening to do rounds of shots and act like fools.*

6. *Walk to the Falls and make bets on when Jorge will cry.*

7. *Yawns, tears, hugs and laughs.*

8. *Walk back to the hotel with a quick stop for sha-warma to soak up all the alcohol.*

9. *Goodnight!*

Amidst all of this debauchery there was a moment where one of us (possibly joking) said that we should call this "RUM FOR THE CURE" and make it an annual thing for us to do, and that, ladies and gents, is when this event was born! Once the weekend was over and we came home, I couldn't shake this great idea that had been brought up. It was fantastic! I began working on putting together a logo for us and wanted to make shirts for everyone as a thank-you but also as a way to bring us closer together. The following year, 2014, marked the first time R.F.T.C. became the reality we know today. I got shirts made for everyone and once we arrived at our usual hotel for the night, I presented everyone with a shirt as a thank-you for keeping me strong and holding me up when I was at my lowest points during treatment.

It has become something to look forward to every year and while it's difficult to get everyone together we always seem to find a way to make it out. What started as a joke between nine guys has become a brotherhood, a secret society filled with "Originals" and "Members," a logo, nicknames, T-shirts, a Facebook page and, most recently, an annual hockey event at the Ricoh Coliseum. We get together not only to have a celebration of life but also to remember those close to us who unfortunately have fallen at the hands of this terrible disease. It is our support group, our show of solidarity and our safe place to air out our grievances with one another. As each year goes by we've added new members and the next step is to see how we can positively give back and still celebrate life. Only time will tell, but for now we RUM FOR THE CURE.

TURN 29
FROM DAMAGED NODES TO TRAVELLED ROADS

I have to thank my brother for giving me the inspiration for this chapter's title. It was his idea to use a play on words about "roads" and "nodes" and I think this sums it up nicely.

One of my biggest frustrations during treatment was the inability to ride my motorcycle. It was July when I had been diagnosed and the riding season had really just begun. I was in the process of getting a new set of wheels that summer and—VROOM!—there it went. My summer of riding was over and I now had other, more important, things to contend with.

I made a promise to myself that once I was done chemo and back in top shape I would do a motorcycle trip every riding season moving forward and thankfully I can say that I have. The voyage did not have to be a long one, I just needed to feel the open road again and that sense of freedom that comes with it. This is a feeling I have never really been able to describe to anyone who does not ride, but I'll give it a try. Imagine the most serene place on earth where nothing matters and every trouble melts away like butter on warm fresh bread out of the oven. Take the most joyful moment you can think of and multiply it by one million and that might explain it.

My first summer out of treatment it was decided that we—my father, uncle and a few friends—would head down to the Adirondack Mountains for a nice four-day trip. New York State has some beautiful roads to ride on and, barring a few turns, bumps and ditches, the trip was a successful one filled with many laughs, moments of uncontrollable joy (crying in my helmet) and great memories to fill my now getting-back-to-normal, chemo-less brain. I would normally take little notes when I ride but decided that I would just let myself enjoy the trip and not worry about diarizing it. I have many pictures to remind me and some cool footage from a digital video camera. Once we returned, I put together a small movie-like trailer for everyone who went on the trip with pictures and footage and called it *Ministers of the Road*. (There had to be a political theme considering the company I was keeping.)

The following summer I was able to check something off of my bucket list when we (pretty much the same people as the year before) decided to tackle Tail of the Dragon at Deals Gap. This is a strip of road on the borders of North Carolina and Tennessee. It is eleven miles in length at an elevation of 1988 feet and is filled with a monstrous 318 turns. It was, in total, a five-day trip and probably one of the most fun rides I've ever had on a motorcycle. I decided I would take daily notes and do a small summary of the trip since it was such a huge deal for me, and I'm glad that I did.

Deals Gap – Tail of the Dragon:

Day 1 Recap – Nine hundred kilometres, a slight detour, a late dinner, a very tall beer, a shot of tequila and the snore machine that is my father...so no sleep last night = Welcome to 'Merica or, more specifically, Winchester, Virginia. Next stop: Blowing Rock, NC...

Day 2 Recap – Eight hundred and fifty kilometres, a fantastic trip through the Skyline Drive, some great footage, no detours, no dinner and best of all twenty-two ounces of beer and an Advil to get me to sleep and no snore machine tonight. Hello Knoxville, Tennessee!

Day 3 Recap – Three hundred and fifty kilometres, "Dragon" slayed, a great ride through the first part of the Blue Ridge Parkway (elevation: 6053 feet), a great dinner and waaay too much tequila consumed! Thanks for the great time, Asheville, North Carolina!!!

Day 4 Recap – Nine hundred and eight-four kilometres, some more awesome riding through the Blue Ridge Parkway, a very nice state trooper who didn't give me a ticket for going seventy miles per hour in a forty-five miles-per-hour zone (Thank you, Officer Johnson) and another fantastic dinner! Almost home but first a well-deserved rest in Washington, Pennsylvania.

Day 5 Recap – Five hundred and seventy-six kilometres, twenty-five minutes waiting at the border, bike switched back into kilometres (hate reading and then converting things into miles) and home safe and sound! Great trip and an approximate total of... wait for it...3700 kilometres in five days!!

This was by far one of the greatest rides I had experienced and the following year I looked forward to another great trip. The next trip was a solo journey for me. I felt that I needed a moment or two alone and while my friends and family were surprised, they just wanted to be sure that I didn't end up having a *Deliverance* moment. (Something about having a pretty mouth...?) I rode the

Adirondacks once again, this time on my own. Along the coast of the south side of Lake Ontario, down to the Adirondacks and then up through to Montreal with a quick stopover in Ottawa to visit family. It was another great trip that reminded me of how precious life is and that we must embrace the wonderful moments it brings.

I realize that none of this has to do with my journey on the Cancer Highway, but life is short and you never know when it will take a turn for the worse, so do the things you love without regret and keep the ones you love close. For in a blink of an eye, it might all disappear.

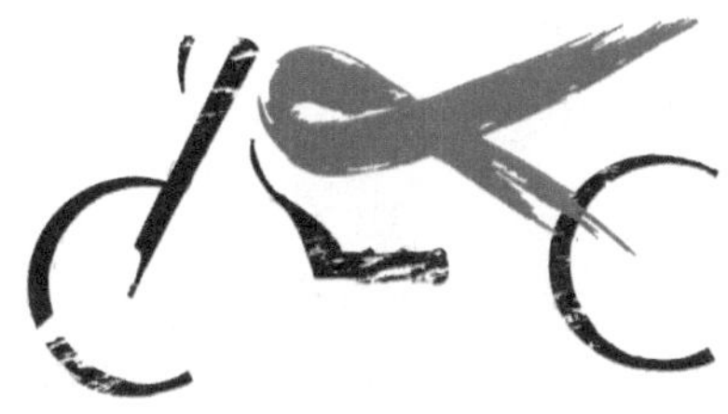

TURN 30
SOMETHING HAS TO GIVE

Relationships are funny things, my friends. One second you feel as if you're on top of the world and nothing can go wrong and then—BOOM!—the weight of the world is on your shoulders and there's no escape from drowning. It's kind of like a mouse in a maze searching after that piece of cheese but never actually being able to find it. They are filled with ups and downs and while this story was about my journey on the cancer cruise ship, there is a component that must be told regarding the demise of a relationship and how the journey may have contributed to it.

To be perfectly clear, this is not a rant or bashing of my former partner in any way, shape or form. These are just my feelings and my interpretation of how things played out in our relationship.

I knew my partner was worried and was struggling to keep a strong face for me at every turn. I wasn't your usual kind of patient and she wasn't the typical partner.

I was: A PAIN IN THE ASS!

She was: A nurse who dealt with critically ill patients all day long at work and then came home to me and my sickness.

It became very hard to separate work and home life. They seemed to be one and the same. Even today, I'm still amazed at how much it impacted our time together.

What started out in April 2012 as a new journey together in our first home with a new dog and our cat, quickly turned into one stressful moment after another that pushed and pulled on the fabric of our relationship to the point of destroying it. They say that time heals all wounds but what they don't tell you is that those wounds need to be addressed to heal and no amount of time will heal a wound that is still bleeding. We spent many moments not talking about issues as my sickness had taken over our daily life. Once treatment was over, I think we both thought things would just go back to the way they used to be but that was never going to be the case. I was a different person. I went in thinking I was invincible and cocky and came out the other end a very different individual.

We attempted to make life normal again but it always felt as if there was an underlying resentment on both sides and, while we tried to make it work, it never really seemed to get back to the way it was. There were visits to couples' therapy, individual therapy, trips, time apart, time together, alone and with friends, family, and it never seemed quite right. It just felt like trying to fit a square peg into a round hole.

I once had a brief heart-to-heart with my nurse and she mentioned to me that many couples that go through a traumatic experience like the one we were going through break up when treatment is over because of the stress and the growth that happens with the patient during treatment. She said that it was a kind of rebirth for most patients—one that, in many cases, leads to a restart.

Maybe it was because I was feeling a constant void in my life and I would do anything to fill it. I would spend my days going to work and then coming home and going off to ride my motorcycle, rehearsing/recording with the band or playing hockey. We once had a conversation and my partner mentioned to me that I was acting like an addict trying to get my next fix, which, in a sense, I was.

I had become addicted to life; I couldn't get enough, and I was hooked. I felt so locked up inside that the minute the cage opened I was out and firing on all cylinders. I didn't want to miss a single moment and while deep down inside I knew this wouldn't last, I didn't care. It was "Vegas or bust, baby!" I was all in, and my relationship was now going to take a back seat. I felt that during treatment I had lost something, so it was now time to get it back.

DQC©
PHOTOGRAPHY

TURN 31
HIS NAME IS...JORGE SOUSA

During my amazing cancer expedition, I had various epiphanies or moments of clarity about life and this disease. I'm left with a proverbial memory "burn-in" of these moments and here are just a few of them:

- Cancer is a shitshow that does not discriminate. It does not care about our religious beliefs, our race, our sexual orientation, or anything else.

- Patients don't all have the same look (frail, thin, bald, etc.) and we unfortunately don't all have the same outcome.

- Treatments feel, in my opinion, counterproductive as the medicine we take not only tries to kill the cancer but, in turn, also kills us.

- The journey beats you and those around you down until you feel as if you can't fight back, but we must stay strong and know that there is always hope.

- There are great people who choose to help others during possibly their weakest moments and, for some, potentially the end of their existence.

- Surround yourself with good people!

- Fight back!

- Stay positive!

- Live and love fully and completely!

When you are fortunate enough to come out on the other side after a lengthy battle with cancer, you look at life in a completely different way. I used to take the little things in my life for granted. Cancer was my wakeup call because the only day I could count on after that was TODAY. I have finally realized that tomorrow is promised to no one.

This journey was cathartic and emotional but I hope that someone, somewhere, somehow has found a glimmer of hope or solace within my words. Know that YOU ARE NOT ALONE!

My name is JORGE SOUSA and I am one of those fortunate enough to say that I am a cancer survivor. This was just a glimpse into my demeanor, psyche and moral sensitivity throughout this battle. Anyone who wishes to connect with me to learn/know more, or if you are looking for someone to speak with about your own journey or the journey of a loved one, please feel free to email me at desolate.jorge.sousa@gmail.com. I am always willing to give back in any way.

ACKNOWLEDGMENTS

You have been a part of something that a few years ago I never would have thought possible and for that I want to start off by saying thank you! You have continuously reached out, helped me make sense of my thoughts and pushed me to continue writing this. As much as this story was about my journey, I feel like it was ours.

I have a laundry list of people that I will forever owe a debt of gratitude and I am humbled and truly appreciate the support, positive vibes, love and well-wishes I received (and continue to receive) directly and indirectly during this crazy battle.

To all the doctors and nurses – I am here today because of you and the care you take with your patients. You give selflessly on a daily basis and I am truly grateful to have had you caring for me during this journey.

To family and friends – You have all had the courage and strength to deal with me and everything calmly in a storm of craziness. Your thoughts, prayers, well-wishes, positive vibes, hugs, kisses (real and digital) kept me going during my darkest moments. We dealt with this the only way we know how…HEAD ON and you kept my spirits elevated through it all.

The R.F.T.C. Crew – You guys have always been there through thick and thin to prop me up and keep me going and there is no way I can ever show how deep my appreciation runs.

My brothers in Desolate Rage – While you guys aren't blood, I consider you family. You guys accept me for who I am and you are the ones who would do anything to see me smile and are there no matter what. When everything went to hell you stood with me without flinching and kept me going.

This hard-hitting ride is over and I have many wonderful memories to remind me of how precious life is and how great the people in it truly are.

In time, a new journey will emerge (I'm sure) with many twists and turns and hopefully I will be able to face it with guns blazing and a full tank.

"LIVE YOUR LIFE LIKE YOU'LL DIE TONIGHT. DREAM LIKE YOU'LL LIVE FOREVER."
– Machine Head